Natural Way To Master Your
Psychology

**Learn How To Analyze
Your Subconscious Mind**

Tyler Leap

© 2016

Table of Contents

Chapter 1

Benefits of Analyzing Subconscious Mind

I'm going to talk about what the subconscious mind is, how it influences your life and the results that you're getting in your life and your success and fulfillment in life. We're also going to talk about how you can start to work with your subconscious mind to get it on board to get you the results that you want.

Subconscious mind is an extremely deep topic that I'm fascinated by. It's also crucial for the results that you are or are not getting in your life.

If you're frustrated with things like losing weight, starting a business, performing well in your job, or anywhere else in your life where you're not getting the results that you want, you have to realize that the most important thing is starting to understand your subconscious mind.

The fact that you're reading this book and you're researching this topic is a good first start. However, I'm going to cover the subconscious mind a lot more in-depth in other books.

Let's break into it.

What is thea subconscious mind? What you have is your conscious mind which is what we tend to think of as our mind. It's us. It's who we are. It's everything that we think and feel throughout the day. It's what we would call "consciousness" or "awareness." That's the conscious mind.

What most people do not understand, unless they've studied this topic and thought about it deeply, is that the subconscious mind is responsible for everything else that is happening in your body and your life. It's responsible for all the behaviors.

The subconscious mind consists of the things that are below your awareness level and below your awareness threshold that are operating on you. These are the habits that you have. These are the beliefs that you have. This is the self-image that you've cultivated and what you think about yourself, your capabilities, your limitations, your weaknesses, and your strengths.

This is also going to include your map and model of reality. It goes deep here. This is basically your model of reality and what you think is right and wrong. The stuff that motivates you on a deep level is all subconscious. We tend to think that that's conscious, but that all sits below the level of awareness unless you've done a lot of introspection and personal development work.

What tends to happen is that the subconscious is driving a lot of what you do throughout your day. I would say that 95 percent of the things that you do throughout your day are done subconsciously or even unconsciously.

When things are happening subconsciously, it means that when you're executing your morning routine or when you've even having a conversation with a friend, you're not breaking a lot of the things and behaviors that are happening there down in your mind and saying, "Okay, I need to pull out the toothbrush, put the toothpaste on it, stick it in my mouth, scrape it around for five minutes, then pull it out and rinse."

You're not thinking all of that. That's just happening spontaneously. In fact, what you're probably thinking about is something totally different while you're brushing your teeth.

You're probably thinking about the fact that you have a big meeting at work coming up and you have to prepare for that or maybe the electricity bill is due or you have to work on your business and there's some problem that you have to tackle. You're probably thinking about something like that versus the mechanics of brushing your teeth.

The question then is – who is brushing your teeth? Is it the conscious you or the subconscious you? If you ponder this and start to notice different areas in your life where stuff is happening spontaneously without a lot of your conscious effort or awareness in the moment, then that is a sign that it's happening from your subconscious mind.

That's what it is. We have habits and we have beliefs and we have everything that's going on in our lives that is coming from an unconscious place.

This is an important idea because this means that if you want to get a change in your behavior or your beliefs or your life and you're not happy with the way that things are running right now, then the real solution, if you want to solve it permanently and get amazing results, is going to happen on a subconscious level and not on a conscious level.

This is simply because your behaviors, which are contributing to the results that you're getting and the action that you're taking, are coming from the subconscious. If you have certain beliefs that are holding you back or certain limitations about who you think you are, your self-image, how confident you are, how good you think you look, or what you think you're capable of or not capable of, it's going to hold you back and you're not even going to realize it.

You can spend years hitting your head against the wall by trying to lose weight, for example, or trying to be more successful in relationships or in dating or trying to start a business and failing at it, simply because you have the stuff below the surface and you don't even realize that it's there.

What can you do about this? The problem is that it is under the surface and it's not something that you can just go in and immediately fix. The other problem is that the subconscious mind doesn't respond well to just a one-time conscious input.

You might think, "The way to fix that is to go to therapy and maybe we'll dig up some stuff in the past about something that happened to me in my childhood, like some traumatic event, and then that will surface and that will clear up and, all of a sudden, I will be better in my relationship or be better at the gym or be better with managing money," or whatever.

While that can happen and that does happen sometimes, generally, the problem is that just knowing about it is not enough. Putting a little bit of awareness on it is a good start. However, the subconscious mind is an animal mind.

You can think of the fact that all animals are operating on a subconscious level. They do have an awareness. They do have consciousness. However, they don't have that pre-frontal cortex-thinking that we tend to associate with normal consciousness.

They're operating more on a subconscious level. It's more instinctual and more behavioral. What they respond to and what response or stimulus that system responds to is carrots and sticks.

It's good at understanding when you give it incentives and you incentivize it again and again. It's also good at understanding sticks and being hit over the head again and again.

That's why, if you've ever had big changes in your life or big transformations, it's usually happened because you've either gotten yourself on board with some sort of inspiring vision and you've drilled that vision into yourself through some sort of process of visualization and that caused a shift in your subconscious or – and this is probably more likely the case if you don't do a lot of personal development work – you tend to go with the negative model.

What happens is that your subconscious is reshaped by hitting your head against a brick wall time and time again until, finally, something cliques clicks and something gives in. What's happening in both of those models is that your subconscious is being retrained.

The important thing to understand here is that that takes time. You cannot simply retrain your subconscious mind with one stimulus. You can't just give yourself one carrot or one stick. You have to do it again and again.

That's why consistency and persistence are key hallmark traits of successful people. They achieve their success by going out there and growing themselves and working on their subconscious whether they realize what they're doing or they don't.

They're working on their subconscious and they're altering it by doing this visualization process and creating amazing visions and goals for themselves. They're repeating them to themselves ad nauseam until they just are immersed in it and believe it. They reshape their beliefs and self-image and are able to go out and do amazing things.

It could also be the other way around where they hit their heads against the wall and they fail again and again and just keep struggling. They keep at it because they're naturally persistent people and have faith. Then some stuff clicks for them and they move on to the next level and evolve. Through that process of persistence, they're able to re-mold their subconscious mind to get to the point where it's doing what they want for them.

That's the process and that's why change is difficult and can take a long time. That's why a simple one-time motivational speech or reading a book one time or going to the gym one time or thinking positively for one day is not going to create a deep and meaningful level of change in yourself.

That's going to take place on a conscious level and it's going to feel nice. You might even be inspired and feel great about yourself for the moment. However, it's not going to be a lasting thing.

Everything about you that's permanent and lasting is embedded deep in your self-subconscious. If you want permanent and lasting results and you want to eliminate some deep-seated negative habits, you have to do the opposite. You have to have some deep-seated positive thoughts and habits that you're constantly think about.

It's a question of positive versus negative patterns. These patterns are etched into your mind. Your beliefs are even deeper because you have the thoughts that you're having and then you have the beliefs that are creating the model of reality.

This is a deep concept. You can do a lot of amazing and advanced person development work when you start to work with this idea and start to use techniques that create these grooves.

You start to align your life with this whole idea that what you're doing to get success is not going out there and getting some external result or taking some action or hitting the gym hard.

What you're doing is working on yourself and the subconscious mind of yours. You're analyzing it and introspecting on it. You're journaling about it and doing the visualizations and affirmations. You're doing various techniques.

Maybe you're going to therapy and you're trying to get stuff to come out and up from your subconscious. Then you're also trying to instill stuff into your subconscious with the conscious mind.

Your conscious mind is limited because you only have so much willpower throughout the day. There's only so much that you can do using your conscious mind. It's only going to get you so far in life.

What you have to do is be smarter than that. You have to start thinking, "I have this limited willpower. How can I not waste it and use it to imprint those grooves on my subconscious mind so that the subconscious mind does all the heavy lifting?"

What's nice is that once you train your subconscious mind in any activity, whether it's a sport, musical instrument, running a business, being good with people and relationships, or mastering your own psychology by eliminating worry and instilling positive thought habits, when you do that, after a while, you build up those habits and it's a relief.

You can actually have some change in your life and you don't need to constantly stay vigilant with it. You can go to the gym and you don't need to always be on guard about falling off track. You can be a little bit more at peace with it because you've built the habit and imprinted that idea into my subconscious. Now you can use that willpower that you have and put it to other purposes.

This is a powerful and advanced-level concept. One of the action items for you, from this book, is awareness. I want you to gain more awareness. I want you to spend a little bit more time, throughout your day, noticing the things that are happening that you're doing. It's the subconscious part of you that's doing them.

Think about that and think about the fact that your subconscious mind could be more aligned with your conscious goals and desires than it currently is.

Chapter 2

What Hidden Thoughts are in Your Subconscious Mind

I'm going to talk about how to get things done.
One thing that I notice looking at people around me is that, generally speaking, people are really bad at generating results. And this is very important if you want to self-actualize. You need to become a results-maker.

I don't know if you realize this, if you've noticed. But the world runs on results, right? Whether it's business, or money, or career, or fitness — or even your internal mood. All that stuff is a result. Everything that you're looking for in life is a result.

So, if you can't do this, if you're not a results-maker, and you don't have this in your pedigree — to be able to go out there and achieve extraordinary results, uncommon results — then, basically, you have a problem. You see this? You see how this is a very fundamental problem?

And most people who are having problems in life, like getting their finances together, or getting their relationship together, or getting whatever other facet of their life together — it's because they are poor results-makers. It's not because they are bad in that one particular facet, although that can certainly be the case. But it's more general than that.

It's like you're bad at making results happen. You're not a results-maker. and you want this kind of pedigree. So that you can say to yourself: "You know, I've made big results happen in the past. Whether it was in my relationship, or with my internal mood, or with my finances, or with whatever. And I can trust myself to make big results happen in the future".

This is like an attitude thing. It's an attitude you take towards life. So, what I want to talk about here is — I want to give you a little bit of deeper understanding of the mindsets and attitudes that a results-maker takes towards life. Why this is important. And then I want to give you a very juicy list of ways that you can adopt some of these results-maker mindsets. I'm going to give you a whole, nice juicy list.

Pursuit The Results

So, when we talk about self-actualizing, when we talk about living up to your full potential, do you realize what that actually entails? That entails getting results. Not just dreams, and ideas, and theories, because — yeah, those things are nice. And you could argue that everything starts as a dream at first.

But the problem is that many people just get lost in the dreams. And the theories. And the ideas. And then they talk a lot of nonsense about what they are going to do with their life. How they are going to change it. Or what they are going to create for themselves. Or how they are going to lose some weight. Or go get married, or whatever.

But then, all that talk and all those dreams — they don't mean anything unless you know how to translate them into the real world. And that's an ability. That's something you train yourself to do. And what's interesting is that modern-day society, in a sense, makes it easy for us to lose sight of results.

Because what you can do is — you can just go with the flow of society. And you can just go get your standard nine-to-five job. Some basic career. Just kind of work that. And live, and survive. And you can even maybe thrive in that kind of environment. Because life's pretty easy these days. It's not like it was ten thousand years ago. Think about what it was like ten thousand years ago.

Ten thousand years ago, you couldn't just plug yourself into the system. Ten thousand years ago, it was like — create results or die. And a good way to prove this to yourself is: try just going on a camping trip for a couple of weeks. Maybe for a whole month. Or, at least do this in your mind if you're not going to do it in practice. Do it in your mind right now.

Imagine you go on a camping trip. And it's just you. You and nobody else. No one to help you. You don't have any food with you. All you have is a tent, a knife, and a gun. That's all you get. Maybe you got a canteen for some water. That's it.

Now, what are you going to do to survive for that whole month? Out there in the wilderness, all by yourself? Well, you're going to have to create some results, aren't you? You're going to have to go, first of all — find some water. Because if you don't get water, within two days you're going to be dead.

So, you got to go find a good, clean source of water. Make sure that it's actually clean. If you find a bad source of water, and drink it — you're going to die within a few days. If you don't find water, you're going to die within a few days. So, there's just that.

Then, you're going to start to go hungry. So, you're going to have to go and hunt using your rifle. Now, you got to actually learn how to shoot the rifle. You actually got to learn how to sneak up on animals, find the animals in the wilderness — because it's not like animals are just running around and waiting for you to shoot them. You got to spot them first, track them down.

And then, after you shoot them, you got to clean them up. Make sure they're edible. You got to use your knife to skin the animal. You got to cook it somehow. You got to start a fire somehow, right? And you don't just have to do that once, but you got to keep doing that consistently.

In fact, you got to probably shoot half a dozen animals a day in order to feed yourself just for that one day. Because hunting requires a lot of expenditure of energy. So, that's just the basics there. But then you also need shelter.

So, you got to build yourself some kind of shelter. Make sure that it's not getting overheated by the heat, by the sun. So it's not getting too cold at night. And you got to manage all of that. And you got to be actually creating a certain result. Because, in the wilderness, if you're not getting the result — then, basically, you're dead. Something's going to kill you at some point.

Now, it was easier to be in touch with that ten thousand years ago than it is now. Because nowadays, if you just let yourself go, society will kind of take care of you. And even in the worst-case scenario, like a homeless on the street, who doesn't have a place to live, still — they have a lot of luxuries these days that you wouldn't have ten thousand years ago.

The Fire Of Reality

So, that's one problem, right? The other interesting facet of this is that I find there's this interesting dynamic going on here of why people are not good results-makers. And it's because they don't hold their own feet to the fire of reality. That's what I call it.

So, what I noticed in myself, especially when I was younger, is that I would come up with cool ideas and dreams for a business that I want to start. Or how my career is going to go. Or for how I'm going to learn a lot of money. Or travel somewhere. Or do some cool thing. So, I would have these ambitions.

But then, what would happen is that I would spend a lot of time thinking about this, and planning it all out. But that was like me living in my little bubble. My fantasy bubble. It wasn't connected to reality in any way. My feet weren't getting held to the fire of reality.

Then what happened is that I was getting older, and older, and older. And I started to get out of college, and I started to go to the job market. Find myself a real job. Actually started paying my bills. That sort of thing. All of the sudden, it's like: "O-oh. Now the rubber meets the road. And now all my dreams are suddenly shattered and thrown out the window. Because there's no way they can work in real life".

Because now, what happens is that the bubble touches the edge of reality. And when it does, it usually bursts. Because the bubble's not strong enough. And so what happens is that you have to scramble, and you have to start to think: "Oh, how do I re-adapt my beliefs and my dreams, and my ambitions to, actually, what will work in the real world?" Because you try to get something to actually work in the real world.

And you discover, like: "Oh, well the marketplace doesn't want this project that I was dreaming up. No one wants to buy it". Or it's like: "Well, I thought I could charge a thousand dollars for it, and it turns out that people don't even want to pay fifty dollars for it. It turns out that people even don't want it for free. Oh — I didn't anticipate that. Oh — that's how markets actually work? Oh good — what am I going to do now?".

And now you have to scramble. And the interesting psychological dynamic here is that it's emotionally disturbing and uncomfortable for us to have our bubbles popped. We don't like it. We like to live in fantasy land. And so, what a lot of people do, I suspect, is that they live in fantasy land, but then they never ground themselves. Because this grounding process — it doesn't just happen once.

You have to keep doing it again, and again, and again, and again. And this is what a really good results-maker is able to do. He's able to hold his own feet to the fire. Or, as the other people, what they are is — they are just dreamers. They are dreamers, and they are big-talkers. And they talk a lot of nonsense — but they don't actually get anything accomplished.

And I think that one of my personal strengths is that I am results-oriented. And for me, this happened, actually — there was like a shift in my life when this happened. Because I used to be a very big dreamer throughout middle school and high school, and into college. And after college, I had to get very serious. Had to start going off on my own, leave the family nest.

And this shift happened psychologically, within me. Where I kind of had to bite the bullet and tell myself: "If I want these dreams to actually get accomplished — if I really value my dreams — then that means I have to be willing to do what's necessary to be done". And that's usually dirty work.

"I have to be willing to get into the mud. Get myself dirty in order to translate the dream into reality." And that translation process — that's a very messy, dirty, emotionally difficult thing to undertake. Because what has to happen is, first of all — you have to be flexible enough to relinquish a lot of your fantasies and beliefs.

Because here's the cool thing about reality — reality doesn't change for you. You got to change for reality. Now, there are, really, two options that you have. One is — you can come up with all these cool dreams and then, when you try to implement them within reality, you see that: "Oh, it's not working". And then you have a choice.

You could say: "Ok, it's not working. So, let me just go and fantasize some more and forget about this whole thing or trying to make my dreams real. Let me just not to that. It's kind of painful. Kind of unpleasant and uncomfortable. I don't want to go through all that". So, that's one option. That's the emotionally-easy option.

Then there's the emotionally-difficult option. Which is to say, and this is the mature option, which is to say: "Man, I was really misguided about my understandings of reality. I thought this thing would fly — it's not going to fly. Not even close. Let me go back to the drawing board. Let me think of a new idea. Let me not only do that, but also let me introspect and analyze my own process."

"What kind of beliefs do I hold about the world, which are making it impossible for me to make this project actually fly in the real word? Oh, yeah, I got a couple of these beliefs. I can see not how those beliefs are probably wrong. But, man, I don't want to give up those beliefs. Oh, man, but I have to give up those beliefs if I want to make this work".

So, basically what happens is that you have to mature. And you have to evolve. And you have to let go of your old dogmas about the way you think things should work. And then, actually, you have to be humble enough to let reality work on you. This is why I call — holding your feet to the fire of reality. And it's an emotionally painful thing. For me, I discovered this when I started to work within the video game industry.

Working Your Way Up

One thing I wanted is to create these cool games. But, you know, creating cool games costs lots of money, takes lots of work. And what I quickly realized is that all my fancy ideas for games that I've been dreaming up for the last five or tens years — a lot of those are not going to fly. And I'm going to have to make a lot of sacrifices to make some of those work, right?

And that's when my face, not just my feet, but my face got smashed into reality. And that was painful. And that was difficult. And it's disillusioning, right? Disillusioning. When people tell you that: "Oh, used to be idealistic, like you, but then, you know — reality showed up and now I have to lower my expectations, lower my dreams and all that stuff".

Well, you could do that. And some people, what they do is that they just keep living in their fantasy bubbles. And they don't actually admit to themselves that all the things that they're fantasizing isn't getting translated into real results.

Stage green is a certain stereotype of people. It's a certain level of psychological development. Actually, it's a pretty high level. Most people aren't even at green.

But the green stage is stereotyped as the hippie, or the new-ager. And what's interesting about these people is that they really have this sense of concern for the world, right? So, their circle of concern increases, so that they don't just care about themselves selfishly. But now they care about other countries, and societies, and other people, and even animals.

So, that's a cool thing. And also, what happens is that they become empathizers. They start actually caring. And they have genuine concern about the emotions, and feelings, and suffering of other people, right? So, these people usually are interested in charitable causes, like saving the whales, and saving the polar bears. And helping poor children in Africa, right? And that's a good intention.

But one of the problems with this stage green is that, even though these people have really good intentions, and the are very idealistic, and they want to come together and share ideas, and they want to talk it out, and they want to come up with a plan for how to live in harmony and in peace, and so that everybody loves each other, right — they are not actually good results-makers.

And so, what happens in practice is that they come together, sit in a circle, and they sing Kumbaya. And they talk about how everyone should live in peace, and everyone should love each other, and how we're going to save the environments, and save the whales, and do all this nice stuff.

But then, in reality, what happens is that you just have that moment, of sitting in a circle. And then everyone disperses, goes home. And nothing actually changes in the real world. So, they are not very good results-makers.

Are you that way in your life? Do you talk a lot of nonsense, but then don't get anything done. Do you have a pedigree of creating results? That's very important, if you really want to create either success or even happiness. You might think that: "Well, happiness doesn't depend on creating all these tangible results". But actually, it does.

And in fact, these green hippie people who like to preach spirituality and how spiritual they are. And who also are very big into relationships — they also talk about how connected they are to everybody else, and they very much values intimacy and relationships, and communication.

Well ,these things: spirituality and relationships — these are actually categories within which it takes serious results-making to get good results. It's one thing to talk about how you're going to have this loving relationship. And then, it's another totally different thing to actually have a loving relationship. And to actually engineer that, to design it. To make it happen.

Because a loving, intimate relationship doesn't happen by accident. That takes a lot of skill to develop that. You need to develop yourself as a human being in order to be able to sustain a really high-quality intimate relationship.

And a lot of times, these hippie people — they might talk about relationships and how great they are. But then, in practice, you take a look at their lives and you see that: "Oh, man, their relationships are bad". Or — spirituality. They might talk about how spiritual they are, and yada, yada, yada. Talk about chakras and energy, and love, and all these fancy spiritual concepts.

But then you actually take a look at them. Are they actually spiritually developed. Do they actually understand? Are they conscious of their own ego? And all the illusions that are happening there? And what you find is that, oftentimes — they are not.

In fact, what they are doing is — they are using all the spiritual talk as a way to muddy the waters. So that they can distract themselves from having to look at the fact that, actually, in reality — they aren't spiritual at all. This is what I mean by holding your feet to the fire.

What you need to do as a results-maker, if you want to really be a results-maker and self-actualize — you need to bite this bullet at some point in your life. And you got to say to yourself: "Man, ok, I can't be one of this people who just dreams messed up and then doesn't make it happen. I got to bite the bullet on this, and I actually got to get humbled by reality".

"Like, if reality wants to beat my face to a bloody pulp, then I'm willing to take those hard knocks. Because that's worth it to me. Because I actually care about getting my dreams realized."

And then you actually got to take those knocks and pay that cost. And what that might mean for you is — giving up some of your very cherished beliefs that you're clinging to. Or reconciling some of the issues you've got with money. Or the way that the economy works. Or the way politics works. Or the way that relationships actually work.

Not your fantasy ideal of how love works, and how everyone should love each other unconditionally. Because that things doesn't happen in real life in an intimate relationship. An intimate relationship is not unconditional love. It's a very selfish kind of love. It's really like a business negotiation.

But do you have the balls to admit that to yourself? To admit that, and then work within that, and then transcend that? That takes some real doing, right? And that requires willingness on your part to take on the burden of expending emotional labor to make this stuff happen. Which is what most people are not willing to do.

Going All The Way

So, instead of talking a bunch of nonsense, what I'd like from you is to actually do the things and ask yourself to get the real results that you want. So, if you're going to start a small business, go start the business. Stop talking about it.

If you want to go earn more money, and take care of your finances, shut up and go take care of your finances. So that actually, the numbers in your bank account are increasing. That's the thing that you should be judging yourself on.

Not how well you can talk. Or how well you can dream some things up. If you want to move to a new country, when you actually move to that new country — that's when it counts. before that, it's just a bunch of talk. Same thing with losing weight. Same thing with your relationships. Same thing with your happiness levels.

Are you actually increasing your happiness levels, or are you just talking about it? Enlightenment — are you really pursuing enlightenment, or are you just talking a bunch of nonsense about enlightenment? You need to stop talking, do less talking and more doing.

And when you do doing, don't confuse just doing for results. There's a very big difference between just doing stuff and getting results. Because you can do certain things that will never generate a results at all. And, in fact, a lot of people make this mistake. A results-maker makes this distinction makes very clear in this mind.

If I'm doing something, and it's not generating results within a week or two, I got to change that thing up. So that I'm doing something else. Kind of — change my approach. Can't get stuck. A lot of people, they get stuck in these cycles where they are just doing stuff they think it's going to produce something later on. And it never produces anything.

And they don't want to change. Because change is emotionally difficult. Not let me make the counter-point. Which is that — some people might listen to this and say: "Ok, but isn't there more to life than just results?"

And the answer, of course, is yes. There is more to life than just results. So, I don't want you to take my point here as being that you got to be this neurotic results-maker. only focusing on results everywhere. No. But first what you got to do is, I think, build a pedigree of creating results.

After you've done that, and you've proven that you're a results-maker, and you've developed that discipline and that skill, and those mindsets — then you can ease off the pedal and maybe sit back, and meditate. Enjoy life a little bit. Don't be so results-focused.

But I think, for most people, what they need more of is — they need more of this results-making mentality. Because the results-making is usually the hard thing. It's the emotionally difficult thing. Just sitting back and relaxing, in a sense — that can be emotionally difficult too, to actually properly relax.

If you're a workaholic type, who's always working his but off, then you probably actually have this opposite problem, Which is that you can't sit back, and your relax and enjoy yourself. So, for you, maybe you got to swing the pendulum the opposite way.

But for many people, that's not the case. So, I'm not telling you here to become a workaholic, necessarily. You don't need to work yourself to death. But you do need to develop this kind of mentality. It's a mentality thing. So, with that said, how do you actually do this? Let me give you a good, juicy list. Here's how a results-maker thinks.

So, the first thing is that you actually have to value tangible results. This is a mindset thing. An attitude thing. So, for example, if you're an employer. And your employees are coming to you with stuff they are supposed to be doing for you, right? You have to be the one that actually sets the standard for tangible results being created.

If you're an employee right now, one thing you can do is, again, you can start to value tangible results. Are the people around you creating tangible results? Are you holding yourself to that standard of "I got to create tangible results, otherwise I'm not really doing anything"? That's the first thing.

The second this is — you actually have to create something. Seems a bit crass and oversimplified, but it really is this simple. Are you a creator in your life? Or you're doing something else? For me — I'm creatively-minded. I'm also project-minded. What this means is I see my life as a series of projects that I'm working on. And I find that this is a very useful mindset for creating results.

Because if you are like an average person, who doesn't thing about their life as a series of projects and, instead, just thinks of it like: "Yeah, I got my job and I'm just going to keep doing that while it pays me money, and maybe later I'll get a new job, and I'll just keep bouncing from job to job, and just survive that way" — if you're that kind of person, you're going to be bad at generating results.

See, the way I think about it is like this: "Ok, I got a project that's due six months from now. I got to release this product. If I create this product, and I release this product, then I'm going to go on and create the next product. Then, maybe I'm going to go create this business. Then I'm going to start a new business two years after that. And so on and so forth.

Those projects are like specific, tangible things I got to put out into the real world. Whether it's a website, a blog, a video, a video course, a set of audios, a book I want to write, or whatever. That's how I think of my life. In terms of these milestone projects. Which I want myself completing every six or twelve months, or so, right?

Some of them are small, and some of them are bigger. But that's important. Start thinking of your life in terms of projects. What are you actually creating in the next six months? Is it a tangible thing? When it's a tangible thing, that means you got to actually make it.

Because then it's very clear in your mind that, if you don't make it within the next six months, you know you failed. Now, if you never set that tangible thing in the first place, then it's like — well, you can't even tell whether you failed or not, because you had nothing you were working towards.

Creating Impact

Another point. Desire to impact people. For me, this is huge. Personally, this is the reason why I want to be a results-maker. Because I want to actually change how people think and what they feel. And I want to change the world.

To have an impact on the world, you need to actually create something. That is the impact. So, by definition, you have to be a results-maker if you want to create impact. Now, for me, that's because I actually want to change people. Or, you know, I want to change something.

Whether it's creating a more beautiful piece of art, or whether it's writing a cool blog post. Or creating a new video that's going to change someone's mind, right? The video has to be created in order for someone's mind to change. Someone's mind is not going to change just from me sitting and dreaming something up.

Most people, though, they don't care about impacting anyone. All they want is a cushy life. If all you want is a cushy life, you're going to be terrible at making results. Because you really don't have a strong enough motivation to create results. When you have a real valid reason to be creating work which is connected to you life purpose, then you can go out there and really make some strong results happen.

Talk Is Cheap

Next point is something that I call "Talk is cheap". And it really is. People tell all the time all the hit they're going to do. I want to start a business" or "Oh, I want start this charity organization that going to transform the world" or "I want to cure AIDS in Africa".

But all this is just talk. It's just talk. One in a hundred people will be serious when they're telling me this stuff. The other ninety-nine percent — they are just jokers. Just talking nonsense. So, in my mind, what I've done a long time ago is — I've totally discounted talk.

When someone tells me they are going to do something, in my mind — it means nothing. It's like empty sounds. You're going to do something? Don't tell me you're going to do something — just go do it.

Don't tell me you're going to lose twenty pounds — go lose the twenty pounds, then come talk to me about it. Don't tell me you're going to write a book — write the book. Then come show it to me. Then we can talk. Oftentimes, talk is just a distraction from holding your feet to the fire.

Nothing But Excellence

Another point is: work for excellence. Value excellence for its own sake. Want to be putting out the best you can be putting out. It's crazy to me, because I worked with contractors sometimes, that helped me do stuff for my business. And I've worked with contractors for a long time in other businesses that I've had.

And basically, they are either writing stuff for me, or doing some coding, or whatever task I have them do. But then, they submit their work and their work is just this sloppy work. No, granted that I don't always pay them that much that they'll be doing the most beautiful work ever.

But still, it's like sloppy work. You'd be ashamed to submit that kind of work to a boss or somebody. It's just work. No excellence is put into it. It's like they don't value excellence. If you don't value excellence, then how can you be a strong results-maker?

Another point is: take personal responsibility for making it happen, whatever it is. Losing weight, starting a business, some project at work, earning more money for somebody, whatever. Personal responsibility has to be taken. You have to believe that it's your job.

Nobody else is going to do it for you.

Stop waiting for somebody else to lead you. To show you the way. To tell you what to do. If there's some initiative at work that needs doing, step up and do it. Take personal responsibility. I always assume that, if I don't get it done, it'll never get done and no one will do it for me. That's like my general operating principle for life.

Whatever it is, I have to do it. Sometimes, I can even get a little neurotic. Where it's even difficult for me to work with people. Because I just tend to assume that they're inherently unreliable. Because a lot of them are. But there's still an art of finding reliable — you can find reliable people. So, don't let that be a limiting belief.

Another important point is: working the big picture. A results-maker is powerful because he has a big picture, high-level understanding of what we're working towards, and why we're working towards it. There's a purpose behind what he's doing.

He's not just doing some menial labor for somebody else, just because he's going to get paid for it. That's a terrible way to go about it.

Instead, it's like he can see, from a thousand foot elevation, what needs to be done and why it needs to be done.

I think that's another attribute that I have that's contributed to my success in life — it's that I'm always looking at the big picture. Why am I doing this? How is this thing going to play into the next thing? And how's that going to connect with my long-term vision for my life and for how I want to impact the world? A lot of people don't think this way. You have to start thinking that way.

Mind The Work Ethic

The next point is work ethic. You got to build a strong work ethic. And that's something that's lacking these days. Because, again, in modern society, especially kids growing up these days — we're so spoiled with all the nonsense that we get. All the free entertainment, and free thing, and free that. Everything's taken for granted.

Just thing back even a couple of generations ago. A hundred years ago. when your great-grandparents were alive. The kind of work ethics that people had back then. Mind-blowing, amazing. Sometimes I read books about successful people in the past. I think about someone like Benjamin Franklin or Nikola Tesla. People that lived a couple of hundred years ago. Thomas Edison. Thomas Jefferson.

What these people were able to accomplish in their lives is amazing. And they had to work through a lot more things than we had to do these days. It was a lot harder back then. But they had these incredible work ethics. They were work mules, these guys. That's rare these days.

It's tough to develop that. Especially in our modern culture. Our culture is very much focused on spoiling us and making us comfortable. And it really devalues work ethics. So, you have to go against the grain on this.

And you have to be willing to use brute force. That's something I've always left open s an option. That, if there's some result that I want to get to, and I can see that I can brute-force my way with work to get to that result — then I'll just do it. I'll gravitate towards doing it.

Whereas, what I see with some people is that it's like: "Yes, we could accomplish this goal by brute force, but, oh, I don't want to brute-force it. Isn't there a shortcut? Isn't there some magic solution? Do I really have to sit there for five hours and hammer on this thing until it gets done? I don't want to do that".

And so, what they say is: "Uhm, let me go look for another approach". And then they never find that approach. And they never get anything done. Now, this is not to say again that you have to be a workaholic and work stupid. No, you work smart.

You don't want to be just working for work's sake and doing bunch of menial labor. But if you can see that menial labor, by doing it for a short period of time, can get you to the next level, then you have to be willing to go there and do it. That's brute force.

Comfort Is A Bad Thing

Next point. Sacrifice comfort. A lot of times, you got to sacrifice some of your own personal comfort to generate some powerful result in life. Maybe you got to stay up late to finish writing this book for the publishing milestone. Or maybe you got to skip your next vacation in order to do something and advance yourself.

Well, are you willing to do that? Or are you living life just for comfort? If your life is lived for comfort, then your life is going to, actually, very ironically, be a very miserable life. because it's like this self-serving, ego-indulgence — its like hedonism. And hedonism, counter-intuitively, doesn't actually produce the greatest happiness. So watch out for that.

Next point, which is a really important one. You have to be willing to change yourself to get the result.

That, to me, is the nutshell of it. Most people are not willing to do this. Most people — they'll go as far as getting up to their edge of their comfort zone and saying: "Ok, well this is the edge of what I could possibly do. So that's it. That's it. I've maxed myself out".

No. The real results-maker, what he does is, he says: "Well, right now I'm only capable of going here. But my result is five steps beyond my current ability level. So what I'm going to do is transform my entire psyche as necessary to get those five steps extra, that I can't get to right now".

Whatever it takes — building skills, reading books, taking coaching, seminars, studying, practicing, research, all that stuff. Not just that stuff. That stuff is basic. That's like a mandatory thing. You got to learn technical skills to get good at what you want to create. I'm talking a bout even going further than that.

Like — dropping entire chucks of belief systems out of your world view. Like, deep psychological changes, right? Changing how you view the entire cosmos. Your thoughts on God and on physics and on science.

All this stuff, I found, has to be changed in order to really become an amazing results-maker.

And it's hard for most people to see that. Why are these changes necessary? These changes seem so deep, and so abstract, and so loosely connected to being able to generate practical results. But for me, it's all interconnected.

For example, if you're a very dogmatic person, if you're not able to be very open-minded, you're going to have a difficult time generating the best results you possibly can. And most people are so dogmatic they don't even understand what the word 'dogma' means.

And they will deny their dogmas till their death. To me, this is ridiculous, right? Because, like I said, a long time ago I made the decision that I'm going to align myself with reality no matter what the emotional cost is to me. I'm not going to try to preserve my ego and make myself more comfortable.

I'm going to align myself with the harshest truths that are out there. Because I now that that's going to, eventually, pay off really big for me. And it has. And it's going to continue to. That's one of my founding principles by which I live life. Which I think that most people don't do. I'm kind of surprised by it, honestly?

Next point: throw yourself into demanding situations. There's nothing like just throwing yourself — launching yourself outside your comfort zone. Think about a military boot camp. This is exactly what it is. You take some soft, new recruits. Throw them into a couple of months of brutal, intense boot camp training. And all of the sudden, they come out soldiers in the end.

And what happens in that process is that their psyche just gets shell-shocked into transforming, right? It's like a total shock to your system. And you have so much emotional pressure on you. Some people break down. Some people lose it. Some people can't handle it. But then, those that do survive the process — they come out much stronger.

And that's what you got to do in your life. So, if you're living that easy, comfortable life that you have been for the last five or ten years, how about throwing yourself into a demanding situation? Such as moving to a new country. Launching yourself into a new relationship. Starting a new business. Or whatever else you can think of like that.

Pick Your "Surroundings"

Next point: be around exceptional people. If you surround yourself with mediocre people, who are not generating any results in life, then you will assimilate their attitudes and mindsets. And you will think that that's normal. Whereas, if you are a results-maker, what you do is — you actually want to distance yourself from those people. Surround yourself with other results-makers.

And then, what happens is that those results-makers bring you up to their level. Because, if you're friends with a person who's able to generate incredible results, you start to see that: "Oh, I didn't even know it was possible to generate results of that caliber. And if that guy could do it, maybe I could do it too? And if this guy could do it, and if that guy could do it, then I could probably do it too". It raises up your expectations of yourself. Important.

The next point is, and I just touched on this, but: starting your own business. I think that nothing holds your feet to the fire more than starting your own business and seeing the brutal realities of the marketplace.

Because, when you first start your own business, you have these fancy business ideas. But then, what happens is that you write up this cool, nifty business plan. But then, what happens is that you actually go and you try to implement it — and it all goes nowhere.

None of it works. No one's willing to pay you a dime. Your marketing doesn't work. You're not able to attract a single client. No one's interested in your stuff — even for free. They don't care. And then, that's when you have that real big eye opener.

It's like: "Oh, I really don't understand how the marketplace works. My understanding of the marketplace is so childish. It has to really mature. And that's where your feet get just burned on that fire. And that burning — that's a good thing.

See, most people, when they feel that burn — they don't like it. It's not comfortable to them. So they run away. And they feel like: "Oh, the burn is bad". But actually, the secret to life is that the burn is good. You have to train yourself to love that burn in a kind of masochistic, sadistic sort of way, right? Just don't take it over the top.

For me, starting my own business was really big. That was the point where I really took on the challenge, bit the bullet and said: "Ok. I'm going to figure it out somehow. And I'm going to take full responsibility".

And the stakes were so high that I had to figure it out. Because, literally, I left my nine-to-five job. And then, what happened was that — if I was going to be earning money, if I wasn't going to be able to attract the clients, and actually get dollars in my bank account — then I would be homeless within a relatively brief period of time.

So, that really lit a fire under my but, and the stakes were high. And when the stakes are that high, then what happens is that you — usually, your ego relents, and it surrenders. And it says: "Ok, I'll change myself to live". So, take that leap if you really want to master results-making.

Memento Mori

And the last point I'm going to say is: think about your death. That's a little odd. "Think about your death? How does that help you to be a results-maker?" Well, for me, very directly. In fact, I found myself thinking about my own death on a daily basis nowadays.

Like, randomly thinking about my own death. How I'm going to die. Like, maybe I'll get killed by a meteor landing and smashing into the earth tomorrow. And I won't even wake up to know — I'll just burn away. Or some nuclear war starts while I'm asleep, and then I never even wake up to see it.

To me, this is important because it shows me how little time I have to get things done. I don't have eternity. I have a very short window within which to make my results happen. So, this makes me focused on generating results, right? My own death.

This is something that most people don't do. They don't really think about this stuff. In fact, they actively try to distract themselves from thinking about their own death. So that they can pretend to have forever to live. And then, when they think that they have forever to live, they don't do anything.

They throw away all their time. Piss away their youth. And then, when they are old and in their sixties and seventies — then they start with all the regrets. And all the things that they should've done when they were younger. And yada, yada — you know how it works, right? Don't fall into that trap. Think about your death often, so that you're reminded of how little time you actually have.

So, that's my list. The point in all this, and what I want you to take away from this book is, simply, that — you need to get off your but. Take action on the things I'm telling you.

Whatever you want — what is it? A career? More money? Relationship? Happiness? Meditate better? Decide the result that you want, make a project out of it, get off your but, start doing it. Hold your feet to the fire. Feel that burn, and learn to love that burn.

If you start applying this stuff in your life, and taking action on it, you're going to become one of the most extraordinary results-makers in your life, that you know. In your whole circle of acquaintances and friends. And the things you're going to be able to achieve, and the satisfaction that you're going to get from being able to achieve it — is going to be remarkable.

It's really — the pinnacle of life is getting there. And I want you to get there. So, there's so much material there. Go check it out. Maybe you're interested in — it can help you to launch yourself into the next level.

Chapter 3
Exploring Subconscious Mind To Create Success

One of the most important ways to grow yourself is to become aware of how your subconscious mind holds you back from greatness. If you think you're free of limiting beliefs, you're kidding yourself. If you think you're going to achieve your dreams without addressing your limiting beliefs, you're kidding yourself. I recently had an epiphany that revealed one of my own greatest limitations, and I want to show you how it unfolded.

A Story About A Mushroom

Recently my girlfriend flew in to visit me from out of town. While cooking for her one night, I sauteed up a batch of mushrooms. While stirring the mushrooms, one of them fell out of the pan and tumbled down to the floor. I immediately, reflexively, picked it up off the floor and threw it back in the pan Eeeeww!! What's worse, I tried to do it on the sly. I knew it was the "wrong" thing to do, but I also felt bad about letting a good mushroom go to waste. Luckily my girlfriend caught me red-handed and called me out on it: "Hey, did you just put that mushroom back in the pan?!" Shamefully I had to confess: "Umm…. Yeaaah?" And that's when it hit me: I have a real problem with money!

Lifting The Veil

What is really going here? Notice what happened here. On the surface is looks like I have a problem with hygiene, but actually, I have a problem with scarcity. I put the mushroom back in the pan because I didn't want to waste it. But, you might wonder, if there were still plenty of mushrooms left in the pan, how important can one freaking mushroom be? But this is a failure to appreciate the depth of the problem. It's not really about mushrooms. It's about my limiting beliefs around needing to be secure. The subconscious mind is very sneaky and operates in illogical ways.

In this case, one mushroom triggers subconscious feelings of money-scarcity even though I own a business, I have zero debt, and I have a large savings. Yet still I get triggered. Can this really be possible? Absolutely! This just goes to show how deep our conditioning and limiting beliefs run. And you're doing the same silly thing in your own life too!

Why So Neurotic

Many people have a bad relationship with money because they spend it too frivolously. But I have the opposite problem: I am too conservative. Now that I'm aware of this, I observe myself very carefully when I'm cooking food. Inevitably food falls on the floor every now and then, and if I'm conscious, I can notice a deep impulse in me to pick it up and reuse it, even though my higher self knows better. Why is this happening? Quite simply, I have subconscious fear of going broke. And this fear drives me to be stingy, conservative, and economical in the most neurotic ways. I have this fear because my childhood was always plagued with money problems. Even though my family was never poor, we always struggled with money. We never had a reliable source of income. The ups and downs of my family's financial situation left a deep imprint in my mind about lack of money and the need to save. This imprint is so strong that even a decade later, after many years of personal development work, I am still emotional triggered by money

Chapter 4
Practical Method How To Get Work Done

Watch Out For Distractions

After this incident with the mushroom, I became very conscious on my limiting beliefs around money. It was like an epiphany. Now that I became conscious, I set up a rule for myself that I will throw out anything that falls to the floor, on principle. Notice that this is NOT a hygiene issue. Hygiene is not as big a factor as it might seem. Human beings can tolerate much more dirt and uncleanliness than most people would believe. The modern world is sanitized to the extreme. It wasn't like that for hundreds of thousands of years of human evolution. I've got nothing against hygiene, but to focus on that would be to miss the bigger point.

Deep Wiring, Deep Unwiring

The problem is that even after you discover your limiting conditioning, like I did in this case, it's still hard to just tell yourself to shut it off. Subconscious conditioning is wired very deep, so it's hard to unwire. You have to do a lot of inner work to unwire it. This takes a level of commitment that few people understand. But this is some of the most powerful personal development work you can do. You have to always be on the look out for how your limiting beliefs manifest themselves, and then as soon as you spot them, you have to commit to fixing them. Do not assume that such a deep issue will spontaneously resolve itself. If you don't take the time and effort to actively weed out your limiting beliefs, they will keep you stuck for life.

Greatness Squandered

This whole problem goes way deeper than just food on a plate or even money. The underlying tragedy is that my neurotic relationship with money keeps me from impacting the world. Because I'm triggered by money, I am too stingy with myself and my dreams. For example, I will hesitate to invest in great business opportunities because I want to feel 100% secure. But in the end this holds me back because not only am I missing out on new sources of income, but I'm actually cutting short my self-actualization. It's funny, but I actually don't value money. I only value money in it's ability to enable me to impact other people and do great work. So ultimately if I'm stingy with my money I will not invest in myself, I will not create the business I want, and I will not live out my life purpose. There is a direct link between my stinginess with food and my inability to live my life purpose. And this have been a recurring theme in my life now for at least 10 years! The whole issue revolves around creating a sense of security. If I can't feel secure, I will never go out there and do the really scary things that I need to do to fulfill my life purpose.

Security As Prerequisite

The human brain is wired in such a way that you can only take on challenge and risk when you feel secure. Psychological studied have demonstrated that security is a prerequisite for risk-taking. The way they prove this is by putting a 2 year old baby in a strange new room full of toys and other interesting objects. If the baby's mother is present in the room, the baby will venture out and explore the space and play with the toys. In this case the mother is simply present. She doesn't encourage or help the baby in any way. If the baby's mother is absent, the baby will cower in the corner and never interact with anything. Why does this happen? Because for a baby, it's mother is the most important thing. If the mother is lost, the baby is screwed. More generally, when a human being feels threatened, survival instinct takes over. All priority is shifted towards establishing security. A human baby doesn't have the luxury to play with toys if its mother is missing. All attention gets hijacked to find the mother. If this didn't happen, it's pretty clear that the baby would be at a huge survival disadvantage. Okay, that all makes sense, but how does this apply to you? Well... You are still that baby! You're just a little bit taller. The moral of this study is: to go out there and create a powerful life, you have to take care of your survival needs. If you don't handle your base needs, they will prevent you from living on your edge.

Chapter 5
How Subconscious Mind Can Hold You Back

Dig Deep And Commit

Be very observant about how your hang-ups cripple you. As we've seen with me, my hang-ups cripple me financially and in business. Where do your hang-ups limit you? Perhaps you have hang-ups around relationships, or fitness, or diet, or career, or education, or socialization. Perhaps someone told you that you were stupid? Perhaps someone told you that you were ugly? Perhaps someone told you that you're a failure? Any one of these can haunt you for life. Take a very honest and deep look inside yourself. Look deep into your past because most hang-ups get created in childhood and early adulthood. Look for ways in which a big childhood block is manifesting itself in your life right now in subtle ways and not-so-subtle ways. I have committed myself to ironing out my hang-ups around money, no matter what it takes, because I know I need to clear that out to move higher. You should do the same Once you uncover your hang-up, you need to commit to ironing it out, otherwise you will remain stuck for the rest of your life. The awesome silver-lining to all this is that right now there are tools and resources available to help you permanently get over any hang-up, no matter how bad you think it is.

The method

Many people have a bad relationship with money because they spend it too frivolously. But I have the opposite problem: I am too conservative. Now that I'm aware of this, I observe myself very carefully when I'm cooking food. Inevitably food falls on the floor every now and then, and if I'm conscious, I can notice a deep impulse in me to pick it up and reuse it, even though my higher self knows better. Why is this happening? Quite simply, I have subconscious fear of going broke. And this fear drives me to be stingy, conservative, and economical in the most neurotic ways. I have this fear because my childhood was always plagued with money problems. Even though my family was never poor, we always struggled with money. We never had a reliable source of income. The ups and downs of my family's financial situation left a deep imprint in my mind about lack of money and the need to save. This imprint is so strong that even a decade later, after many years of personal development work, I am still emotional triggered by money.

Watch Out For Distractions

After this incident with the mushroom, I became very conscious on my limiting beliefs around money. It was like an epiphany. Now that I became conscious, I set up a rule for myself that I will throw out anything that falls to the floor, on principle. Notice that this is NOT a hygiene issue. Hygiene is not as big a factor as it might seem. Human beings can tolerate much more dirt and uncleanliness than most people would believe. The modern world is sanitized to the extreme. It wasn't like that for hundreds of thousands of years of human evolution. I've got nothing against hygiene, but to focus on that would be to miss the bigger point.

Deep Wiring, Deep Unwiring

The problem is that even after you discover your limiting conditioning, like I did in this case, it's still hard to just tell yourself to shut it off. Subconscious conditioning is wired very deep, so it's hard to unwire. You have to do a lot of inner work to unwire it. This takes a level of commitment that few people understand. But this is some of the most powerful personal development work you can do. You have to always be on the look out for how your limiting beliefs manifest themselves, and then as soon as you spot them, you have to commit to fixing them. Do not assume that such a deep issue will spontaneously resolve itself. If you don't take the time and effort to actively weed out your limiting beliefs, they will keep you stuck for life.

Greatness Squandered

This whole problem goes way deeper than just food on a plate or even money. The underlying tragedy is that my neurotic relationship with money keeps me from impacting the world. Because I'm triggered by money, I am too stingy with myself and my dreams. For example, I will hesitate to invest in great business opportunities because I want to feel 100% secure. But in the end this holds me back because not only am I missing out on new sources of income, but I'm actually cutting short my self-actualization. It's funny, but I actually don't value money. I only value money in it's ability to enable me to impact other people and do great work. So ultimately if I'm stingy with my money I will not invest in myself, I will not create the business I want, and I will not live out my life purpose. There is a direct link between my stinginess with food and my inability to live my life purpose. And this have been a recurring theme in my life now for at least 10 years! The whole issue revolves around creating a sense of security. If I can't feel secure, I will never go out there and do the really scary things that I need to do to fulfill my life purpose.

Chapter 6
One Of The Most Powerful Methods To Reprogram Your Unconscious Mind

Security As Prerequisite

The human brain is wired in such a way that you can only take on challenge and risk when you feel secure. Psychological studied have demonstrated that security is a prerequisite for risk-taking. The way they prove this is by putting a 2 year old baby in a strange new room full of toys and other interesting objects. If the baby's mother is present in the room, the baby will venture out and explore the space and play with the toys. In this case the mother is simply present. She doesn't encourage or help the baby in any way. If the baby's mother is absent, the baby will cower in the corner and never interact with anything. Why does this happen? Because for a baby, it's mother is the most important thing. If the mother is lost, the baby is screwed. More generally, when a human being feels threatened, survival instinct takes over. All priority is shifted towards establishing security. A human baby doesn't have the luxury to play with toys if its mother is missing. All attention gets hijacked to find the mother. If this didn't happen, it's pretty clear that the baby would be at a huge survival disadvantage. Okay, that all makes sense, but how does this apply to you? Well... You are still that baby! You're just a little bit taller. The moral of this study is: to go out there and create a powerful life, you have to take care of your survival needs. If you don't handle your base needs, they will prevent you from living on your edge.

Commit

Be very observant about how your hang-ups cripple you. As we've seen with me, my hang-ups cripple me financially and in business. Where do your hang-ups limit you? Perhaps you have hang-ups around relationships, or fitness, or diet, or career, or education, or socialization. Perhaps someone told you that you were stupid? Perhaps someone told you that you were ugly? Perhaps someone told you that you're a failure? Any one of these can haunt you for life. Take a very honest and deep look inside yourself. Look deep into your past because most hang-ups get created in childhood and early adulthood. Look for ways in which a big childhood block is manifesting itself in your life right now in subtle ways and not-so-subtle ways. I have committed myself to ironing out my hang-ups around money, no matter what it takes, because I know I need to clear that out to move higher. You should do the same Once you uncover your hang-up, you need to commit to ironing it out, otherwise you will remain stuck for the rest of your life. The awesome silver-lining to all this is that right now there are tools and resources available to help you permanently get over any hang-up, no matter how bad you think it is.